199 Ways to Make Your Good Marriage Great or Your Bad Marriage Better

Romance and improve your marriage today!

Richard W. Linford

199 Ways To Make Your Good Marriage Great

or Your Bad Marriage Better!

Sweetwater Book Company
First edition

ISBN 1-57574-018-4

Imprint Linford Corporation

Foreword

I first wrote this concept as "Twenty Ways to Make a Good Marriage Great" which was published in the *Ensign* magazine, December 1983. My wife and I have been married for 44 years.

Following is a 30 question test. Answer yes or no to each. You may want to write a Y or N beside each question.

1. You spend at least 30 positive minutes with your spouse each day other than the time you spend in bed together?

2. You are your spouse's best friend?

3. You have amorous love for your spouse?

4. You help your spouse each day?

5. You do your share of the work in your home?

6. You work together?

7. You track your finances together?

8. You have a "mutual" set of written goals?

9. You are courteous to your spouse?

10. You respect your spouse?

11. You pay careful attention to personal hygiene daily?

12. You work at keeping yourself fit?

13. You are tidy and orderly?

14. You work at improving your living environment?

15. You have positive physical contact with your spouse each day?

16. You hug daily?

17. You kiss daily?

18. You have physical relations on a reasonable schedule?

19. You are kind in all your interactions with your spouse?

20. You are free of personal addictions?

21. You listen to your spouse?

22. You don't interrupt your spouse when he or she is talking?

23. You are free of mental and physical infidelity?

24. You respect your spouse's opinion?

25. You forgive your spouse?

26. You compliment your spouse?

27. You attend Church together?

28. You pray together?

29. You protect your spouse from harm and accident?

30. You are happy with your marriage as it is?

Notice that all 30 questions focus on you and not on your spouse. If you can answer all thirty questions with a yes, you need no improvement. If you need some improvement, read the rest of this book and consider those suggestions that fit your marriage situation.

1. Acting … because the love you have in your marriage is not static but living and needs daily care and nourishment. Love is demonstrated by your actions. In a great marriage love is a helping verb not a noun. Love is something you give and share. Love is a form of work.

2. Adam … because he stood by Eve in what can be a lonely and dreary world.

3. Addictions as not acceptable … because addictions to drugs, alcohol, tobacco, pornography, and misuse of food are destructive to your marriage relationship.

4. Amour … because amour means Cupid and love and amorous love is an integral part of a good marriage.

5. Anger? No! ... because anger is the source unkindness and physical and verbal abuse. Anger is the antithesis of a kind and loving relationship with your spouse.

6. Avoiding those things that are bothering your spouse? Yes! ... because you control how you look and what you do and say ... because emotional connections or intimate flirtations or relations with others more often than not get in the way of your intimacy with your spouse ... because uncouth manners or lack of hygiene can stand between you and a great relation with your spouse ... because you really do know what bothers your spouse and you can do something about it.

7. Belittling? No! ... because belittling your spouse tears down and diminishes both you and your spouse.

8. Best friend … because your spouse can be your best friend and any other "best friend" can detract from your marriage relationship. When your best friend is your spouse, life is beautiful.

9. Breakfast … because breakfast, and even breakfast in bed, can say you care enough to get up and go to the effort … but only if your spouse wants to be awakened. Breakfast at a restaurant can work as well.

10. Budgeting … because tying down your income and expenses and setting financial goals puts you in the same boat rowing together in the same direction toward financial stability.

11. Calendaring ... because as you review and calendar your week together, you can know who has to be where and when, making it possible for you to work together to accomplish what needs to be done. Planning helps family life run smoothly.

12. Caring for your spouse's family ... because enjoying their company, praying for them, serving them, being with them, and overlooking differences tends toward peace and happiness between you and your spouse not to mention your spouse's family.

13. Charity ... because charity "suffereth long, and is kind; charity envieth not; charity vaunteth not itself, is not puffed up. Doth not behave itself unseemly, seeketh not her own, is not easily provoked, thinketh no evil; Rejoiceth not in iniquity, but rejoiceth in the truth; Beareth all things, believeth all things, hopeth all things, endureth all things. Charity never faileth." (1 Corinthians 13:4-8)

14. Chastity ... because chastity is your commitment to have intimate relations only with your husband or wife to whom you are married.

15. Children ... because having and rearing and loving children and enjoying your grandchildren builds great value in your marriage.

16. Chocolate ... because chocolate can be a language of love.

17. Church ... because attending church, temple, synagogue, or mosque together gives your marriage higher tone and purpose.

18. Cleaning the house and yard and car together … because neither of you is maid or butler or gardener for the other.

19. Commitment … because "I do" means you decided and pledged and committed your love for each other.

20. Communication, communication … because talking things out is life blood to a great relationship while silence causes marriage anemia.

21. Community service … because giving to others gives back. Both husband and wife are enriched for the service either gives.

22. Complimenting ... because honest, fair, kind compliments every day are endearing ... because words of approval are words of love ... because you can compliment your spouse verbally or by email or by card ... because by complimenting your spouse you help lift her or him to higher, better, more capable levels ... because the world is harsh and your approval and compliments minimize fear, frustration and anxiety.

23. Concerts ... because the symphony, a rock and roll band, a YouTube date to watch favorites provides common, memorable musical experiences that bind you together.

24. Confidence ... because most everything can work out all right if you trust. Be worthy of the confidence placed in you by your spouse.

25. Contributing to your spouse's emotional bank account ... because daily deposits to your spouse's emotional well-being help build balances sufficient to support withdrawals.

26. Controlling how you argue ... because setting ground rules about how you argue, helps to ensure that your arguments will not be critical, divisive, or hurtful ... because each person should have opportunity to state his point of view in a peaceful, calm setting ... because reasoning together is so much better than arguing.

27. Controlling your words and tone of voice ... because even when you have a difference of opinion, you can use words that contribute to the overall health and satisfaction of your marriage. Angry words, loud and harsh words, are divisive and hurtful. Soft words engender love.

28. Controlling your spouse? No! ... because controlling another person is abuse and steals his or her agency and freedom.

29. Counseling ... because a good, insightful counselor can help you see things as they really are ... because good counseling beats divorce a million times.

30. Courtesies … because saying please and thank you, not interrupting, not doing all the talking, maintaining the highest standard of good manners, opening the car door for your spouse, shows respect and continues your courtship.

31. Courting … because courtship is the glue of love, binding the two of you together.

32. Covenant relationship … because keeping your marriage covenants to your spouse and to God is part and parcel of integrity and love.

33. Creativity? Certainly! … because creative activities add fun and joy to your relationship.

34. Criticizing? No! ... because criticism, including so-called constructive criticism, is very harmful to your relationship. If things really do need to change for the better consider approaching the matter in kindness as "I would appreciate it if ..." and "I feel that ..." as opposed to "You are ..." or "You always ..." or "You never ... ."

35. Dating weekly ... because going to a favorite park, a concert, the library, the gym, a ball game; or staying home for dinner or a movie, or a mutual hobby keeps vitality in your relationship.

36. Debt payoff ... because paying down principle on your mortgage avoids interest ... because paying off credit card and other debts does the same thing ... because interest never sleeps and can destroy you and your marriage hence the wisdom of avoiding as much debt as possible.

37. Differences overlooked … because differences can be used to divide the two of you. Enjoy his or her differences as well as similarities, if you would be unified.

38. Discussing … because questions like "How was your golf game?" and "How was choir practice?" and "Is your throat still soar?" and "How was your day?" and "How are your employees?" and "How is your sister?" and "What can I do to help you?" show that you care and demonstrate that details about his or her life are important to you.

39. "Dissing" your spouse? No! Not when you are alone … Not in public … because whenever you put down your spouse or speak ill of your spouse you not only damage your relationship, but also you damage your image and your relationships with others … because gossiping about your wife's or husband's negative characteristics or actions telegraphs loudly to all that you lack respect and love for your spouse … because airing your grievances in public is like hanging your dirty wash out for everyone to see.

40. Divorcing only as an extreme option! … because divorce most often creates more problems than it solves and this is especially true when there are children involved.

41. Encouraging … because praise, love, and concern make both the hard times and the normal times much easier.

42. Faith in each other … because faith is confidence and trust in one another – the glue of marriage.

43. Fair … because being unfair to your spouse is unfair.

44. Family … because the family is fundamental to a stable society … because family is a singular source of joy and happiness in a troubled world.

45. Family home evening on Monday night or a night of your choosing … because this custom in The Church of Jesus Christ of Latter-day Saint (Mormon) is one we can learn from – a custom that involves setting aside one special night each week to spend time with your family … a time of fun, games, food and learning.

46. Family prayer … because the family who prays together stays together.

47. Food ... because great food prepared by the two of you and served at home or found in a favorite restaurant can also be a language of love.

48. Eating together not alone ... because taking the time to sit down and eat together provides a setting in which the two of you and your children share your life experiences and engage in the family bonding process.

49. Emails ... because an email love note goes a long way to smooth hurt feelings and strengthen your relationship.

50. Emotionally faithful to your spouse … because you are emotionally unfaithful to your spouse if you engage in face to face or online Internet intimacies with another person that should be reserved for your spouse.

51. Eros … because physical love in marriage is important to its success.

52. Eve … because she stood by Adam in this lonely and dreary world.

53. Expectations specifically communicated … because unless you specifically share and focus and frame your expectations together – such as where and when you are going on vacation, or whether you are going to attend Church together, or how you want to honor or discipline one of the kids, or expectations about physical relations, or what you would like for dinner – your marriage camera will continue blurry and out of focus.

54. Expenses discussed … because money discussions help ensure each of you is in agreement with any expenditure over pre-agreed limits and amounts.

55. Family … because family is God's way of continuing the human race and blessing His children.

56. Fidelity and faithfulness to your spouse ... because complete fidelity and faithfulness in thought and action are honest ... because fidelity values your spouse ... because infidelity and unfaithfulness are dishonest, painful, unkind and unrighteous – because infidelity is cheating and devalues your spouse.

57. Financial review ... because daily, weekly, monthly, annual financial reviews keep you on the same financial track.

58. Fitness ... because working at being physically fit means a more healthy "You" and a more healthy "You" should please both your spouse and yourself.

59. Fixing one another? – because fixing doesn't work and never will work -- because fixing is not loving; it's fixing.

60. Flowers and candy … because white, red, pink or yellow roses, carnations, orchids, or living plants can be a language of love. Your spouse's favorite candy bar won't hurt the relationship either.

61. For better or worse … because it is unrealistic to think that all days will be better or worse.

62. Forgetting slights – because slights remembered accumulate in the memory and strain the marriage bond.

63. Forgiving one another ... because as you forgive your spouse God will forgive you ... because forgiveness creates peace of mind ... because things not forgiven create resentment ... because offenses create bitterness ... because your spouse isn't perfect and neither are you ... because each spouse offends the other spouse at one point or another ... because forgiveness creates a climate of freedom conducive to greater emotional intimacy.

64. Friendships you can rely upon ... because as a couple it is important to have good friends you enjoy and trust ... because you need to take initiative and be good friends if you would have good friends.

65. Fun ... because what you do for fun together softens stresses, disappointments, and sorrows and is fundamental to happiness in your marriage.

66. Games ... because games help to lighten your mental and physical burdens.

67. Gardening together ... because there is something better tasting about the fruits and vegetables the two of you plant and tend and harvest.

68. Gentleness ... because anger, compulsion, force, bad temper, and tantrums are sandpaper to your relationship.

69. Getting good out of your marriage ... because as a practical matter the more good you give to your marriage the more good you get out of your marriage.

70. Gifts on occasion ... because a note, a needed item, a more expensive gift at special times, but mostly gifts of time and self show you love each other.

71. Giving ... because what you give returns to you "good measure, pressed down and running over." (Luke 6:8)

72. Goal setting ... because setting goals at an annual retreat in the mountains or at the lake or ocean, in your living room or kitchen or den makes sense ... because mutual goals give direction and are catalyst to couple unity.

73. God the Father worship ... because He loves and blesses you and your spouse.

74. Golda … because Golda loves Tevia and answered his question. Golda: "With our daughters getting married, and this trouble in the town, you're upset. You're worn out. Go inside. Go lie down. Maybe it's indigestion." Tevia: "Ah, no, Golda, I'm asking you a question. Do you love me?" Golda: "You're a fool. Tevia: "I know. But do you love me?" Golda: "Do I love you?" Tevia: "Well?" Golda replies: "For years, I've washed your clothes, cooked your meals, cleaned your house, given you children, milked your cow. After years, why talk about love right now?" Tevia: "Golda. The first time I met you was on our wedding day. I was scared. I was shy. I was nervous." Golda: "So was I." Tevia replies: "But my father and my mother said we'd learn to love each other and now I'm asking, Golda, do you love me?" Golda: "I'm your wife." Tevia: "I know but do you love me?" Golda says: "Do I love him?" Tevia says: "Well?" Golda says: "For years, I've lived with him, fought with him, starved with him, for years my bed is his. If that's not love, what is?" Tevia says: "Then you love me?" Golda says: "I suppose I do." And Tevia says: "And I suppose I love you, too. It doesn't change a thing but even so after years, it's nice to know."

75. Gratitude and thanks ... because little things are the big things in marriage ... the sincere "thank you" ... the "I love you" ... the little acts of love, kindness, and appreciation.

76. Grieving together ... because inevitably someone you know will be injured, hurt, sick, or die ... because businesses sometimes fail, accidents happen, and jobs are lost.

77. Happiness In your marriage ... because happiness is your choice ... because happiness in your marriage is a process not an event ... because you can choose to make your marriage happy.

78. Helping … because your spouse shouldn't have to clean-up or prepare meals or wash the dishes or vacuum or garden or do a myriad of things alone.

79. His or her needs first … because your needs ought to be second … because your marriage is not "my" marriage singular; it is "our" marriage plural … because it isn't about what you can get out of your partner; it is what you can give to your partner.

80. Hobbies together … because bowling, golf, tennis, walking, running, gardening, and reading together keep you together.

81. Honesty always ... because lying to your spouse destroys trust.

82. Honoring God ... because the couple who honors God is honored by God.

83. How can I help you? ... because this is one of the most endearing powerful questions in the language.

84. Humility ... because being humble builds a foundation of true love while pride, egotism, and ill will destroy love.

85. Humor ... because being able to see the humor in a situation goes a long way toward peace and healing.

86. Husbands love your wives! Wives love your husbands! ... because the Apostle Paul's statement in Ephesians 5:22-32 is still valid. "Wives, submit yourselves unto your own husbands, as unto the Lord. For the husband is the head of the wife, even as Christ is the head of the church: and he is the savior of the body. Therefore as the church is subject unto Christ, so let the wives be to their own husbands in every thing. Husbands, love your wives, even as Christ also loved the church, and gave himself for it; That he might sanctify and cleanse it with the washing of water by the word. That he might present it to himself a glorious church, not having spot, or wrinkle, or any such thing; but that it should be holy and without blemish. So ought men to love their wives as their own bodies. He that loveth his wife loveth himself. For no man ever yet hated his own flesh; but nourisheth and cherisheth it, even as the Lord the church: For we are members of his body, of his flesh, and of his bones. For this cause shall a man leave his father and mother, and shall be joined unto his wife, and they two shall be one flesh. This is a great mystery: but I speak concerning Christ and the church. Nevertheless let every one of you in particular so love his wife even as himself; and the wife see that she reverence her husband."

87. Hygiene daily if not hourly … because nobody wants to kiss or hug bad breath, body odor, unshaven, shabbily dressed or unclean.

88. "I am sorry!" said quickly … because pride refuses to say "I'm sorry" … because pride sucks the "love" out of love … because refusal to admit you are wrong is immaturity … because "I'm sorry helps your husband or wife forgive you … because "I'm sorry" repairs hurt feelings … because by being the first to say "I'm sorry" and make peace you can mitigate or erase ill will.

89. "I love you!" … because saying "I love you!" at least once each day brings tenderness and security to the relationship … because if you do not tell your spouse you love her or him, he or she will not know … because usually your love is not obvious so you need to state it often … because saying those eight letters and two spaces will hopefully help you hear them in return.

90. "I need you!" ... because these words generate confidence ... because they tell him or her you cannot imagine living without them.

91. "I understand!" ... because understanding is an expression of love.

92. Ice cream ... because ice cream is happy.

93. Important matters and activities together ... because discussing important things together builds unity ... because doing things together builds unity ... because doing things together as often as reasonable makes sense.

94. Interruptions as taboo … because interrupting when he or she is talking is unrefined not to mention unkind.

95. Intimacy … because intimacy is not just a small bite of the apple, it is sharing the seeds.

96. Jesus Christ … because He is the Prince of Peace and living His teachings ensures peace, kindness and love in your relationship.

97. Joy in the journey … because you are joined together for the journey … because making your journey joyful is your choice … because it is up to you.

98. Kindness ... because no kindness to your spouse goes unrewarded ... because kind words are for happy as well as stressed conditions ... because sarcasm, unkind jokes, put downs, and verbal abuse at the expense of your spouse are wrong.

99. Language that is clean ... because conversation laced with swearing or taking the name of God in vain is unrighteous, and destroys good feelings.

100. Laughing together daily ... because laughing alone is lonely.

101. Learning from each other ... because your spouse can teach you much if you will allow it.

102. Learning together … because reading to each other, discussing ideas, taking a class together, are bonding and fun activities.

103. Learning to love and stay true to the person to whom you are married … because he or she is the person who brought you or accompanied you to the marriage dance, and he or she is the person with whom you should dance and go home.

104. Letters … because the art of writing great love letters has been lost and ought to be revived.

105. Life … because a child's life is sacred and marriage is alive and neither ought to be aborted.

106. Listening … Not only to what is said, but also to what is meant … because listening is one of the languages of love.

107. Love … because love in several different languages is amour (Spanish and Portuguese), amore (Italian), amour (French), kjaerlighet (Norwegian). liebe (German), liefde (Dutch), milosc (polish) … because one of the greatest things a father can do for his children is love their mother while one of the greatest things a mother can do for her children is love their father … because the greatest thing a dad and mom can do is love and care for their children.

108. Love at home … because "There is beauty all around when there's love at home." (Words from the Latter-day Saint hymn, "Love at Home.")

109. Love expressed today … because love expressed tomorrow may be love expressed to late.

110. Loving your spouse … because life is short and fraught with peril and you do not know when she or he might unexpectedly be called home or incapacitated … because your children will grow up and leave. So and love each other at every stage and at every age.

111. Loving with all your heart ... because it is one of God's commandments: "Thou shalt love thy wife [thy husband] with all thy heart, and shalt cleave unto her [him] and none else." (Doctrine & Covenants 42:22)

112. Lustful desires? No! ... because lust is sin ... because pornography and lust devalue your spouse and damage intimacy ... because lust sends a signal to your spouse that you are using your spouse and are ambivalent about your marriage.

113. Marriage? Yes! ... because marriage between a man and a woman is ordained of God.

114. Marriage Commitment for always ... because marriage does not have to be just a civil 'til death do us part' commitment. Consider the Latter-day Saint doctrine and tradition wherein marriage is for "time and eternity."

115. Money ... well earned, saved and invested by the two of you.

116. Money ... wisely spent by both of you.

117. Movies, DVDs, and music that are decent and enjoyable ... because that way the two of you watch and listen only to the best and you have no regrets.

118. Music … because great music can be a language of love.

119. Needs spelled out in detail … because your needs can be met if you tell your spouse what they are … because your spouse probably isn't a mind reader.

120. Negative? No! … because negative thoughts, words and actions are irritating and erode your good relationship.

121. Negativity? No! … because a negative marriage is painful … because as you think about, dwell upon, and repeat that which may be negative and wrong, the negative and wrong eclipse the positive and good in your marriage.

122. Negotiating! Yes! ... because compulsion and force don't work ... because negotiation is an expression of practical wisdom and kindness.

123. Obeying the law ... because broken laws cause serious stress and broken marriages.

124. Odd and even days ... because one of the best ways to solve marital differences is to let him choose on odd days and her choose on even days ... because that way he gets to make the decisions and run the remote on his day and she gets to make the decisions and run the remote on her days.

125. One flesh … because once married that is what you are – one flesh.

126. Order … because it is painful to live in a disorderly house or relationship.

127. Painting and fixing up … because by working together to improve your living environment you are more comfortable with each other.

128. Partners and partnership … because a king or queen with servants and the feudal system never did work.

129. Passion … because your marriage will be much more positive if there is passion in the relationship.

130. Patience and long-suffering regardless … because you are not perfect either … because most tardiness, forgotten favors, thoughtless remarks, and impatience can be overlooked and easily forgiven.

131. Peaceful relationship … because peace is worth the price.

132. Peacemaker … because being ambivalent or a war-maker is opposite to being a peacemaker.

133. Phone call daily to touch base and show you care … because unless you make the effort how will your spouse know you really do love and care?

134. Planning together … because daily or weekly planning meetings keep the two of you on the same page and eliminate surprises … to discuss the calendar, talk over needs and problems, and decide priorities and next steps. (You may wish to write decisions in a journal, including your goals and discussion topics.)

135. Please and thank you … because please and thank you are two keys to a happy marriage.

136. Pornography? No! … because pornography is infidelity and destroys trust and love.

137. Positive reinforcement ... because negative reinforcement does not work.

138. Praising ... because in dealing with your spouse, or for that matter anyone else, you get what you praise and you lose what you criticize ... because your spouse will tend to repeat an action that generates praise ... because your honest, specific praise creates good feelings between the two of you.

139. Prayer night and morning to say thanks, to ask for help in your marriage and family, to worship together ... because prayer enlists God's love and power in behalf of you, your spouse and your marriage ... because prayer works. It has been said that "The object of prayer is not to change the will of God, but to secure for ourselves and for others blessings that God is already willing to grant, but that are made conditional on our asking for them. Blessings require some work or effort on our part before we can obtain them. Prayer is a form of work, and is the appointed means for obtaining the highest of all blessings." (King James Bible, LDS Bible Dictionary, p. 53)

140. Principles ... because successful marriages are established and maintained on principles of compassion, faith, forgiveness, love, prayer, repentance , respect, and work ... because decisions in marriage should be made based on reason and principle not on blind emotion.

141. Priority ... because your marriage ought to be your number one priority before money, business, sports, friends, cars, personal projects,   entertainment, and anything else, except God.

142. Problem management ... because there will always be problems and many of them can never be resolved completely. Manage your problems so they don't manage you.

143. Providing … because you need to use your combined talents and resources in providing for each other.

144. Purity … because purity is defined as a pure heart and pure hands and absence of pornography or lust in any fashion.

145. Questions that are kind … because kind questions like "How was your day?" or "How do you feel?" or "What do you think is the right thing to do?" show you care; while questions like "Where have you been? Or "Why did you buy that?" or "What have you been doing?" or "Why are you doing that?" can be unkind and controlling.

146. Quiet ... because you can make a major improvement in your marriage simply by being quiet ... because stillness is the source of peace ... because by being still and holding hands and listening you establish that deep romantic, compassionate connection between the two of you.

147. Reading out loud each evening or morning ... because reading articles or books of common interest aloud will increase your knowledge and create a foundation of things you both know and can discuss.

148. Recreation ... because a great marriage should include planned and unplanned vacations, sports, and entertainment activities.

149. Refraining from whatever you ought to stop doing ... because the key to your better marriage, yes the key to your great marriage, might be as simple as refraining from: TV watching, so much time spent on your hobby or interest, computer games, computer use, Internet surfing, working late or overly long hours, flirting, touching, hugging, kissing, and spending time with friends and relatives, alcohol or tobacco, perhaps prescription or other drugs ... because even though breaking old habits might seem hard, the improvement in your marriage can bring a higher level of personal and marital satisfaction.

150. Renewing your marriage vows ... because such can restate and reinforce your marriage covenants and commitments to each other.

151. Respect … because respect for each other is essential to a happy marriage.

152. Respect for life … because abortion is about babies not just about the mother and father.

153. Respecting privacy … because respect for the opinions, ideas, and privacy of your spouse generates reciprocal respect … but most of all because respecting your spouse's privacy is right.

154. Robert Browning … because he received from Elizabeth Barrett Browning (1806-1861) perhaps the greatest love line of all time "How do I love thee, let me count the ways!" in the following poem:

How do I love thee? Let me count the ways.

I love thee to the depth and breadth and height

My soul can reach, when feeling out of sight

For the ends of Being and ideal Grace.

I love thee to the level of everyday's

Most quiet need, by sun and candle-light.

I love thee freely, as men strive for Right;

I love thee purely, as they turn from Praise.

I love thee with a passion put to use

In my old griefs, and with my childhood's faith

I love thee with a love I seemed to lose

With my lost saints, -- I love thee with the breath,

Smiles, tears, of all my life! – and, if God choose,

I shall but love thee better after death.

155. Romancing ... because romance is ardent, emotional, and a loving attachment or involvement between a man and a woman ... because romance is emotional love in the marriage relationship.

156. Scheduling get away time for intimacy ... because life is extremely busy and everything else expands to erase the opportunity for intimate moments.

157. Scripture reading each day together ... because scriptures are the source of inspiration for yourself and your marriage ... because scriptures help you become more spiritual.

158. Secret to a happy marriage? ... because it is not in finding the right husband or wife, it is in learning to respect and love the husband or wife you have.

159. Security systems that protect your marriage ... because you need to be careful of forces and persons that work at tearing your marriage apart ... because together you need to be wise and talk through and agree in advance on how you will handle situations if people are threatening your marriage.

160. Selfless giving ... because each of you ought to give 100-percent to your marriage.

161. Serving your spouse as you serve yourself ... because he or she in large measure is the mirror image of yourself.

162. Service daily ... because otherwise time for loving service will pass you by!

163. Sexual relations ... because intimate relations are important to a good marriage.

164. Sharing feelings in a kind way ... because feelings shared in kindness tend to foster a loving relationship.

165. Shopping together ... because shopping together can be fun.

166. Sickness and health ... because you are in this marriage for the long haul.

167. Slights forgotten and forgiven ... because slights tend to be remembered while kindnesses tend not to be remembered as well ... because slights that are not forgiven fester.

168. Sleeping ... because getting more sleep is said to contribute to a happy marriage.

169. Smiling ... because smiling makes most everyone happy including your spouse.

170. Sports ... because golf or tennis or hiking or bike riding together can be enjoyable and a means of drawing closer together.

171. Spouse or child abuse of any kind? No! ... because love is the higher and only way ... because physical and or verbal abuse of any kind is unkind and immoral and illegal. Abortion is the ultimate form of child abuse.

172. Supporting ... because each of you deserves the support of the other when it comes to your church or community or work assignments and righteous goals.

173. Surprises of the right kind … because the right kind of surprise is endearing … because spontaneity can be a good thing.

174. Taking your spouse for granted? Absolutely not! … because you need to be aware and appreciative of energy expended in your behalf.

175. Talking … face to face because face to face the two of you can discuss the day and say "I love you" and enjoy a hug … because talking together even about easy or tough matters can be a language of love.

176. Talking less ... because listening to your spouse is a language of love ... because listening to your spouse honors and affirms your spouse ... because you strengthen the connection between the two of you when you listen.

177. Television set in your bedroom? No! ... because television in your bedroom distracts and takes the focus off of the two of you.

178. Television shows and movies and audio you both enjoy ... because why watch alone if you can watch together.

179. Tevia ... because Tevia loves Golda.

180. Thank you … because these two words make you both feel appreciated.

181. The greatest marriage … because this ought to be your goal.

182. Things that hurt your marriage gotten rid of today … because it is important to get rid of substance abuse, financial irresponsibility, anger, thoughts or actions of infidelity, and pornography … because it is important to cut your TV watching, time at work, hobby and sports time, and spend time with your spouse.

183. Threatening spouse and marriage? No! … because threats cause your spouse to fear for the future … because threats injure your spouse and your children in emotional, psychological, and physical ways.

184. Time and energy committed ... because having a better marriage takes a lot of time and energy.

185. Together ... because you can do most important things together.

186. Too much time away from your spouse and kids? ... because too much time away from home, too much time with your hobby or at your computer or at work, to much time with work colleagues or friends, too much time nursing an addiction, is too much time away from your spouse and children ... because too much time away sends a message to your spouse and kids that you do not care that much about marriage and family.

187. Touch … because touching is a language of love.

188. Traveling together … because traveling to fun places on vacation or work assignments will bring you closer and develop unity.

189. Unity … because disunity is no fun at all.

190. Verbalizing your feelings … because if you don't talk about it he or she will not be able to help or adjust or act upon it.

191. Winning life's battles together ... because going it alone is a loser.

192. Wants ... because your spouse not only has needs but also wants ... because focusing just on his or her needs leaves a great deal of joy and satisfaction out of your marriage relationship.

193. What you want and need ... because what you want and need must be said in specific words your spouse can understand ... because it's that old "mind reading" problem again.

194. Words that are soft, kind, and gentle … because soft, kind, and gentle words are the words of tenderness, compassion, sympathy, empathy and love. "A SOFT answer turneth away wrath: but grievous words stir up anger." (Proverbs 15:1)

195. Working together … because caring for a garden, painting a bedroom, washing the car, scrubbing floors, building a piece of furniture, writing a poem, team teaching a class, serving in the community together will draw you closer together.

196. Worshipping together … because the couple who worships together stays together.

197. Writing down your marriage goals … because writing your marriage goals is a first step toward making them a reality.

198. You are beautiful [or handsome] to me … because "you are beautiful [or handsome] to me" makes your love more beautiful.

199. Your marriage can be long lasting and great … because all it takes is you're long lasting commitment. Your marriage can be great … because you have your choice and the power to make your marriage great!

Footnote 1

Twenty Ways to Make a Good Marriage Great

By Richard W. Linford

Richard W. Linford, "Twenty Ways to Make a Good Marriage Great," *Ensign*, Dec 1983, 64.

1. *Night and Morning Prayer ...* to say thanks, to ask for help in your marriage and family, to worship together.

2. *A Weekly Planning Meeting ...* to discuss the calendar, talk over needs and problems, decide priorities and next steps. (Write decisions in a journal, including goals and discussion topics, and reasons for each.)

3. *A Daily Phone Call or Personal Conversation ...* to say "I love you," to touch base, to discuss the day, to show you care.

4. *A Weekly Date ...* to a favorite park, a concert, the library, the gym; or staying home for a candlelight dinner, a game, or a mutual hobby.

5. *Patience Regardless ...* of missed meals, tardiness, forgotten favors, a thoughtless remark, impatience.

6. *Daily Service ...* helping with house or yard work, mending a piece of clothing, taking a turn with the sick baby, fixing a favorite meal. (*Write it down. Do it!*)

7. *A Budget ...* to tie down income and expenses, help set financial goals, and give you control over your finances.

8. *Listening ...* not only to what is said, but also to what is meant.

9. *Regular Attendance ...* at church—and where possible—the temple.

10. *Daily Scripture Reading ...* to learn the gospel, to receive inspiration for yourself and your marriage, to become more like Jesus.

11. *Working Together* ... caring for a garden, painting a bedroom, washing the car, scrubbing floors, building a piece of furniture, writing a poem together, team teaching a class.

12. *Forgiving Each Other* ... always learning from each other, trying a different way, being the first to make peace.

13. *Courtesies* ... like saying please and thank you, not interrupting or belittling, not doing all the talking, continuing the niceties of courtship.

14. *Soft and Kind Words* ... of tenderness, compassion, empathy.

15. *Learning Together by* ... reading to each other, discussing ideas, taking a class.

16. *Respecting* ... opinions, ideas, privacy.

17. *Supporting Your Spouse's* ... Church callings and righteous goals.

18. *Caring for Your Spouse's Family by* ... enjoying their company, praying for them, serving them, overlooking differences.

19. *Occasional Gifts* ... such as a note, a needed item—but mostly gifts of *time* and *self.*

20. *Loving with All Your Heart.* "Thou shalt love thy wife [thy husband] with all thy heart, and shalt cleave unto her [him] and none else." (D&C 42:22.)

Footnote 2
Twelve Alphabetical Marriage Love Languages

Take a few minutes and prioritize them for you and for your spouse.

1. Courtesies
2. Good food
3. Forgiveness
4. Friendship
5. Fun activities
6. Listening
7. Physical relations
8. Service together
9. Talking together
10. Time and attention
11. Touch
12. Worshipping together

For you

1.
2.
3.
4.
5.
6.
7.
8.
9.
10.
11.
12.

For your spouse

1.
2.
3.
4.
5.
6.
7.
8.
9.
10.
11.
12.

Footnote 3
Marriage Love Statements

1. I promise I will keep my marriage covenant with you

2. I will be charitable and kind to you

3. I have confidence in you

4. I will be courteous to you

5. I will continue our courtship

6. I love you

7. I love our family

8. I love your family

9. I forgive you

10. Will you forgive me?

11. You are my best friend

12. I am committed to be gentle with you

13. I promise to and I do give you all that I am and have

14. I am glad we have mutual goals

15. How can I help you

16. Let's worship together

17. I see the humor in this situation

18. I am very careful about my hygiene

19. I am listening to you

20. We can work this out together

21. Would you like to choose on the Odd Days and I'll choose on Even Days

22. I will work at being patient

23. I'm sorry

24. I love to hold you and I love to have you hold me

25. I will say please

26. I feel peaceful when we pray together

27. I am committed to work it out

28. I am committed to decide matters based on principle

29. My priorities place you at the top of my list

30. I am committed to provide for you

31. I respect you

32. I am committed to work at making my words gentle

33. I love it when there is romance in our relationship

34. I am committed to protect you and make you feel secure and safe

35. I am committed to exercise self-control when it comes to our relationship

36. I enjoy serving you

37. I enjoy serving others with you

38. Our physical relations are a great part of our marriage

39. Thanks

40. I love your smile

41. I am committed to spend the time needed to make our marriage great

42. Thank you

Footnote 4
Marriage and The Church of Jesus Christ of Latter-day Saints (The Mormons)

1. I am member of The Church of Jesus Christ of Latter-day Saints and am not in the least shy about sharing my religion and my belief in eternal marriage with you.

2. I believe we are spirit children of God.

3. I believe we lived prior to mortality and had our same identity and personality.

4. I believe we came to mortality through the birth process in order to experience mortality and learn to distinguish between right and wrong, good and evil, light and darkness, health and sickness, pleasure and pain.

5. I believe we continue to live as spirit children of God after death.

6. I believe that at some point in the future we will be resurrected.

7. I believe a couple when sealed together in a Latter-day Saint temple is sealed together as man and wife for eternity.

8. If you want to find out more about eternal marriage click on

9. www.lds.org and

10. www.mormon.org.

Footnote 5

Postscript

My wife and I have been married for 44 years. We have a number of children and grandchildren. I work at being a good husband, father, grandpa, and neighbor. I am a Christian -- an active member of The Church of Jesus Christ of Latter-day Saints (Mormon) and served in the Church as a lay bishop and a member of several stake presidencies. I am a businessman, attorney at law, writer, artist, and sometime golfer and was chairman of a multi-county Red Cross board and state chairman of The National Conference of Christians of Jews and on the NCCJ national board for many years.

We are children of God our Heavenly Father. I dedicate this small work to my family and to you regardless of your religion or beliefs. "Be not afraid" and "be of good cheer" are words of Jesus Christ I find especially comforting. I wish you great health, happiness, and prosperity!

Richard Linford

Footnote 6

Other books by the author

Would Jesus Christ Do That? is the first question! What Would Jesus Do? is the second question! (Christian Conduct)

Andrew Chipman's Christmas Angel (Life after Death)

The Young Marine and The Snow (Light and Darkness)

Stop Strolling Around Naked In Your Business Empire Like "Alittle Kingly" (Business Turnaround)

The Jesus Christ Papers Volume 1: The Many Witnesses That "He Lives!" (Witnesses of Christ)

These can be ordered at www.amazon.com. Type in the book title or author's name Richard W. Linford.

Websites and a Blog you may find interesting: www.lds.org and www.mormon.org. Blog: http://jesus-isthechrist.blogspot.com/

199 Ways to Make Your Good Marriage Great or Your Bad Marriage Better

Romance and improve your marriage today!

Richard W. Linford

www.ingramcontent.com/pod-product-compliance
Lightning Source LLC
LaVergne TN
LVHW081325060426
835511LV00011B/1868